D0509337

DEEP

EAST

TEXAS

DEEP

EAST

TEXAS

Photography by David H. Gibson

LONGSTREET PRESS
Atlanta, Georgia

This project was underwritten by the *Longview News-Journal*, The Texas Eastman Division of Eastman Chemical Company, and Stephen F. Austin State University.

Published by LONGSTREET PRESS, INC.,
a subsidiary of Cox Newspapers,
a division of Cox Enterprises, Inc.
2140 Newmarket Parkway
Suite 118
Marietta, Georgia 30067

Photographs Copyright © 1993 by David H. Gibson

All rights reserved. No part of this book may be reproduced in any form by any means without the prior written permission of the Publisher, excepting brief quotations used in connection with reviews, written specifically for inclusion in a magazine or newspaper.

Printed in the United States of America

1st printing, 1993

ISBN: 1-56352-117-2

This book was printed by Arcata Graphics, Kingsport, Tennessee
The text was set in Adobe Garamond
Separations by Advertising Technologies Incorporated, Atlanta, Georgia

Book and cover design by Jill Dible

Frontispiece: *Road, Harvey Creek*

Dedicated to my parents,
Margaret and Harry Gibson

FOREWORD

The Piney Woods of Deep East Texas may seem a great distance in space, time and culture from New England's Walden Pond, but David Gibson has brought a Thoreau-like sensitivity and observation to the subtle, rich and sensual landscape of eastern Texas. He is not a native of the region, but especially over the last five years he and his wife, Lorine, have made repeated visits exploring this land and have come to appreciate its quiet beauty. Like Walden Pond, the landscape Gibson has photographed is not grand or imposing. Even its most distinctive feature — the surreal, swampy Caddo Lake — does not offer dramatic vistas, but instead envelops the visitor in an almost womblike enclosure of lush plants and water. Like most of Gibson's subjects, the lake is a landscape not to look at from a distance, but to experience from a boat or the shore's edge under a canopy of trees dripping with vegetation.

The East Texas landscapes Gibson has photographed are human scale, and he makes us feel a part of this special place. This is a significant distinction because landscape photographers are commonly more attracted to grandiose terrain like Yellowstone and the Grand Canyon, neglecting less dramatic land closer to home.

It is important for Gibson that the land he photographs is accessible; most of his subjects are easily visited public lands and preserves. Although people are not directly depicted, his photographs often include evidence of human activity in roads, fences and building ruins. People are part of the cycles of nature Gibson records, and there is a sense of optimism in the plantings of daffodils and narcissus outlasting not only the occupation of homes, but blooming long after the buildings have disappeared.

Gibson's photographs teach us to look for and appreciate the simplest detail in the natural landscape. His work makes us aware of the delicate beauty in the chaos of the interlocking branches of young trees or the sculptural magnificence of a massive old stump. We learn to look closer and longer and understand the revelations that different light and seasons can bring.

The East Texas landscape is cherished by its residents, but because it is less imposing than a national park, it is easier to take for granted — or even neglect and lose. Gibson's photographs are free of polemic conservation messages, but he cannot help but be aware of the changes he has seen as freshly-cut trees are trucked away and old-growth forests are lost. Many of the landscapes he has photographed have been preserved simply because they were in low-lying flood plains, or for some reason were difficult to convert to "practical" uses. Some of his more serene photographs were made in Harrison Bayou adjacent to Longhorn Ammunition Plant, but Gibson heard the thundering sounds of the firing of rockets being dismantled as part of the post-Cold War.

As David and Lorine Gibson have come to explore and cherish East Texas, his photographs have reflected that affection. And in deciding to share this experience with others, we can hope that similar experiences will be available to all of us long into the future.

Thomas W. Southall
Curator of Photographs, Amon Carter Museum, Fort Worth, Texas

PREFACE

It is with great pleasure that the three Cox Newspapers that cover East Texas, *The Longview News-Journal*, *The Lufkin Daily News*, and *The Daily Sentinel* of Nacogdoches, present this book, DEEP EAST TEXAS, with its extraordinary photographs of our region.

Although it is the lushest region of Texas, Deep East Texas remains the state's best kept secret. It is a land of stately pines, hardwoods, lakes grand and small, wisteria and honeysuckle. East Texas provides balance to the rugged sagebrush, cactus canyons and vast prairies so often associated with the image of the state. Since my first acquaintance with East Texas, coming to work at the *News-Journal* in 1979, a dream has persisted: find a way to reveal to others this unbridled natural beauty. So it was with enthusiasm that we moved forward in the fall of 1992 when Dallas photographer David Gibson agreed to author the first publication with that single purpose.

Gibson's photographic talent is unquestionably equal to the task at hand. In DEEP EAST TEXAS he reverently unfolds for viewers the intimate details a casual observer would miss. Gibson isolates for us images that form the pertinent pieces of this mystical landscape. These photographs reflect his love for this land, and tell of his patience for the smallest detail and grandest sweep. He presents it all with fresh cadence and ancient richness.

To celebrate this region is a task befitting the newspapers which serve it. Only once in a blue moon, however, is a dream so fulfilled. Revel in this book and you will know Deep East Texas as it is: splendid, lush and mysterious.

For their counsel and support throughout this project, I would like to thank fellow publishers Bill Martin of Lufkin and Glenn McCutchen of Nacogdoches. Thanks also should go to author Laurence C. Walker and museum curator Thomas W. Southall for their writings in this book on East Texas forests and Gibson's photographic technique.

Retta Baker Kelley
Editor and Publisher, *Longview News-Journal*

A NOTE FROM THE PHOTOGRAPHER

Deep East Texas is an old, quiet land. Ancient trees, winding roads, moss and vines offer a sense of time-lessness. A mysterious and almost mystical beauty prevails. Much of the region is defined by this sense of peace and tranquility. It is a wonderful challenge to try to make photographs expressive of this place.

I have been drawn to this land since 1970, when I discovered Caddo Lake. Later, I became familiar with the area around Longview, Marshall, Jefferson, Dangerfield, Pittsburg and Gilmer.

In 1992, at a show of my photographs at Stephen F. Austin State University in Nacogdoches, I met Retta Kelley, an SFA regent and editor and publisher of *The Longview News-Journal*. Retta said the newspaper would be interested in publishing a book of photographs on East Texas. The boundaries emanate from Longview and would be Interstate 30 on the north, Jasper on the south, east along the Louisiana border and west at a north-south line through Tyler. The Piney Woods of Texas form the content of this book.

With a new mission, I expanded my photographic exploration to Nacogdoches, Jasper, Zavalla and Lufkin. I discovered special, almost secret places — with incredible details — throughout this region.

These photographs represent to me a sense of this remarkably intimate landscape. The images were made in parks, along county roads and on the land of new friends made as I researched this book.

Working in the landscape, I feel the continuum of activity — sound, repetitions of patterns and forms, variations in scale and duration. It is a constant process of experiencing the unexpected. It is like listening to music with its structure of sound forming and unfolding during performance. The best photographs seem to have this same sense of passage.

First, there was an emotional response to circumstances. Walking in the woods, I heard a humming sound that became more intense as I moved closer to it. Sunlight filled the blossoms with glowing highlights. There I found bees involved in their work. A breeze carried the freshness of spring and new growth. This is the kind of experience that moves me; a pageant of light, sound and smell.

Over and over I sense this Deep East Texas land is about trees. My first impression of the land was the striking similarity to the rolling hills of my home in Kentucky. I felt the power of tall pines and saw the exotic sculptures of cypress trees draped in Spanish moss. Somehow the land felt like Kentucky but with trees imbued with a special magic.

Events are all around us in nature and are sensed in so many ways. I try to create relationships in a photograph that can impart, and perhaps communicate a sense of experience. The wonder I have found has its source in nature.

David H. Gibson

ACKNOWLEDGMENTS

The creation of this book depended upon the fine support, guidance, and introductions of friends and people of East Texas. Included are the people that made the difference:

. . . . .

Retta Kelley, editor and publisher of *The Longview News-Journal*, whose vision created the context for the work to exist in this form.

. . . . .

Eloise Adams, Stephen F. Austin State University Gallery Director, who introduced my work to the region.

. . . . .

Special thanks to those who helped allow us to discover the special places:

Rosa & Chuck Finsley who first took us to Caddo Lake.
Ted Doremus who shared the Wild Azalea Canyon.
Ned Fritz and Larry Shelton allowed us access to the remarkable Grass Lake.
Dr. Scott Beasley, Forestry Department, Stephen F. Austin State University for allowing access to
 the Experimental Forest.
Forester Tom Brantley for arrangement and guidance in Harrison Bayou, special management area
 within the Longhorn Army Ordinance Depot.
Jim Neal, Texas Parks & Wildlife.
Neal Thompson, Jasper Fish Hatcheries.
John Conner, Director of Parks, Nacogdoches, Texas.

. . . . .

Jack Keever, freelance writer from Austin, whose editing skills make the words work.

. . . . .

Thomas Southall's astute help with the tough choices and the sequence of the photographs.

. . . . .

Jay Dusard's advice in the fine tuning of the images.

. . . . .

Kevin & Cheryl Vogel, Valley House Gallery, whose belief in the work has set the stage for access. Their quiet, experienced council has been a factor at every juncture.

. . . . .

Lorine, wife, friend and partner, through it all.

INTRODUCTION

Two centuries ago, pioneers waded the Sabine River east of present-day Milam to continue their journeys on the *Camino Real*, a roadway blazed in 1691 that would stretch 540 miles to the Rio Grande. Pausing at the river long enough to be baptized into the Roman Catholic faith, pioneers followed the ruts of the road westward through the dark and dank forests of Deep East Texas. A few sojourned in this land of lush vegetation. Others proceeded to the Spanish missions at San Augustine and Nacogdoches, while some folks left the woodlands for the shortgrass prairies of the Spanish colony surrounding San Antonio.

Those who remained in these forests of tall pines and broadleaf trees used 14-pound axes to cut virgin stems of loblolly and shortleaf pines as well as bald cypress for houses. Spanish moss draping from trees served for mattress stuffing and sewing thread. Occasionally squatters sectioned a white oak for barrel staves to hold whiskey distilled along the creeks. Barrels of red oak stored flour and sugar.

Persimmons and plums from the woods provided fruit, locust pods served the need for beans, while walnuts and hickory nuts, pounded, boiled and strained, earned the name *milk of honey*. Rich as fresh cream, the oily liquid added sweetness to hominy grits and cornbread. Basket weavers utilized the bark of young shoots of the redbud, and boiled wild black cherry bark provided delicious tea.

While some homesteaders passed through at what would become Pendleton's Ferry, others entered Spanish, and later Mexican, territory via Blue Elbow, the swamp along the lower Sabine, north of today's city of Orange. Dodging cottonmouth moccasins in dugout canoes shaped from bald cypress logs at the river's edge, the pioneers paddled eastward to a woodland of loblolly pines and a variety of hardwood species. Soon they came upon vast expanses of longleaf pines, the stringlike needles singing tunes to the cadence of the wind. In the geological past, these sandy lands were coastal beaches.

A little more to the west lay the Big Thicket, a dense jungle of pine and deciduous trees that shed their foliage annually. For men running from the law or a lady, this lair of the black bear, with cavernous dens of rattlesnakes, was an ideal hideaway. According to a folklorist of these haunts, the rattlers grow so old they sprout whiskers.

A few citizens would follow the route of botanist Thomas Nuttall, passing through Arkansas territory on a well-traveled Indian trail and entering Texas from the north. On this trail, they often confused the Red River with other waterways to the south. One of the more southern streams is Big Cypress Creek, its water and sediment flowing into Caddo Lake, the South's largest natural lake. Southern bald cypress and tupelo gum dominated this impenetrable wetland until the U. S. government dynamited a "raft" of logs that dammed the river and constructed ditches for transportation routes. In time, water lilies invaded and other aquatic plants migrated to the lake. Leave Caddo, and one promptly encounters pineries and poor lands of scrub oaks and hickories.

A century would pass before harvests of the Texas pineries began in earnest, with the rhythm of the crosscut saw and the whine of the circular saw. Lumbermen arrived in Texas about 1900, after forests in the Northeast and the upper thirds of Michigan, Wisconsin and Minnesota had been depleted.

Still recovering from the Civil War, the nation needed lumber for homes, schools and factories, crossties on which to rest its coast-to-coast rails, and gum naval stores for paints and ammunition. Cordwood was needed to fuel furnaces, steamboats and locomotives. And a new paper industry required fiber from forests. Woodworkers lived with their families in box cars in company towns. Others found shelter in canvas tent cities. The more fortunate lived in mill towns, riding the tram rails in the wee hours and returning home carrying the lantern atop the last load of logs long after dark.

World War I hastened the harvest of the virgin forest. England's prime minister insisted he did not need more of our Army's men to finish off the Kaiser's forces, only "a bridge of ships" to transport material from American factories to the shores of Britain and France. The general who completed construction of the Panama Canal was enlisted to manage the building of the bridge. When timber cutting went too slowly, he complained to the lumbermen that "birds are still nesting in the trees which must go into the lumber out of which to build ships." The lumber barons, a bit more optimistic, bragged "that in 72 hours they could shoo the birds, cut the trees, mill the lumber, and have it at dockside.

Among the 84 vessels completed by Armistice Day, 1918, was the *War Mystery,* launched at Orange as "the largest wooden ship that ever took water." At the same time, the military bought 17,000 carloads of southern lumber to build temporary military quarters.

Fifteen years later, the southern forests were no more. Cutover forests of stumps were now to be sold to the U. S. government "to protect the navigability of navigable streams" and, under a later law, to ensure a future wood supply for the nation. Mid the Great Depression, in 1935-36, some 600,000 acres of Texas industry lands were purchased for an average of $5.20 an acre; some brought as little as $2 an acre. These cutover, burned over, over-grazed barrens became the four national forests which some people today like to imagine are virgin forests that escaped the pioneers' axes.

To understand the change over 50 years, we need to consider the ecology of these woodlands. How did the forest become what it is?

As the 15 million acres of East Texas' commercial forest lands lay bare, owners happily sold their holdings. Millmen assumed the soils would never again bear merchantable timbers. They lacked an understanding of the ecological relationship of the forests they had harvested over four decades.

In the early 1900s, oxen and machines dragged the logs to streams or to steam-powered loaders that lifted the heavy timbers on to log cars pulled by gear-wheel locomotives. American Indians — Caddoes, Alabamas, Coushattas, a few Cherokees — helped fashion the forests encountered by settlers. The Indians burned the forests with regularity, exposing their enemies as well as wildlife. These fires consumed leaves on the ground and opened the canopy of foliage as trees died from the heat. Seeds from the southern pines, coming to rest on the newly exposed mineral soil, would germinate. Thinning the canopy by fire also allows abundant sunlight to reach the ground for growth of Texas' pines. Where protected from adversaries, such as uncontrolled wildfires, grazing cattle and piney-woods' creatures that thrive on roots, the million seeds that gave birth to ten thousand seedlings on an acre would naturally thin as individual trees express dominance. Perhaps a hundred trees per acre reach maturity. In the virgin forest, less than a dozen of the oldtimers, extending into three centuries, would typify the pine stands lumbermen entered.

What species grew in association with the conifers in these old-growth forests? Mostly oaks and hickories grew in the upland shade and American beech, river birch and southern sugar maple along streams. Many other species entered the forests as hitchhiking seeds hanging to the fur of animals; as seeds passed in bird droppings; as nuts, the shells softened by acids in animal stomachs; and on the wings of winds. Other broadleaf species arise as sprouts from roots and stumps of felled trees. As the pines pass from the forest in a hundred years or so, broadleaf trees of beauty, but limited utility, capture the site. The hardwoods remain in control until fire, hurricane winds, insect or disease epidemics, or the loggers' tools prepare the land for the next rotation of pines. Neither herbicides nor the swing of an axe can halt this march: natural process will continue.

In the magnificent forests of Deep East Texas, lovers of the land and its abundant resources find a panorama graced with the finest species for mankind's use, the finest soils in which to grow them, and the finest climate to enhance their vigor. What a blessing.

Laurence C. Walker

· · · · ·

Readers who wish to pursue the history, utilization and rejuvenation of southern forests through the periods of the explorers, pioneers, lumbermen, boat builders and foresters are directed to the author's The Southern Forest: A Chronicle, *published by The University of Texas Press, Austin, Texas, 1991.*

DEEP

EAST

TEXAS

1

Fall Forest, Harvey Creek
Angelina National Forest

2

Lyric Tree, Jackson Hill Park
Angelina National Forest

3

Angled Tree
Douglass

4

Tree, Fox Place
Karnack

Maples
Biloxi Creek

6

Road
Harrison County

Pine Grove
Marshall

8

Stark Trees
Chireno

9

Daffodils
Karnack

10

Narcissus and House
Oak Ridge

11

Sycamore
Nacogdoches

12

Edge Trunks, Boggy Creek
Sam Rayburn Reservoir

13

Cypress Trunk
Big Cypress Bayou

14

Vine and Pine
Stephen F. Austin Experimental Forest

15

Grass and Reeds
Grass Lake

16

Patterns with Pine Cone and Willow Leaves
Sam Rayburn Reservoir

17

Pine Needle Shroud, The Tol Barret House
Nacogdoches

18

Fern Bog
Loco Bayou

19

Bank, Stagecoach Road
Marshall

20

Forest Floor
Angelina National Forest

21

Lizard's Tail
Grass Lake

22

Maypop
Angelina National Forest

23

Azaleas in the Rain, Wild Azalea Canyon
Temple Inland Forest

24

Thistle
Angelina National Forest

25

Dogwood
Jasper

26

Red Maple
Angelina National Forest

27

Pine Chapel, Christian Cemetery
Nacogdoches

28

April Morning
Nacogdoches

29

Dogwood, Wild Azalea Canyon
Temple Inland Forest

30

Light Splash
Harrison Bayou

31

Magnolia and Palmetto
Jasper

Church
Caddo Lake

33

Cypress Trees and Reflections
Big Cypress Bayou

Mill Pond
Caddo Lake

35

Cypress Knees, Mill Pond
Caddo Lake

36

Cypress Sentinels, Mill Pond
Caddo Lake

37

Mill Pond Shore with Water Lilies
Caddo Lake

38

Button Bush Stump, Mill Pond
Caddo Lake

Moss Fabric, Mill Pond
Caddo Lake

Knee Reflections, Mill Pond
Caddo Lake

Seven Cypress Trees, Mill Pond
Caddo Lake

42

Caddo Stillness, Mill Pond
Caddo Lake

43

Bush Island
Caddo Lake

44

Tree Trunk and Reflections
Big Cypress Bayou

45

Water Oak and Cedar
Marshall

46

Road
Angelina National Forest

47

Lost Dogwood
Stephen F. Austin Experimental Forest

48

Spring Forest Tapestry
Jasper

Morning Forest
Angelina National Forest

Low Lands
Stephen F. Austin Experimental Forest

51

Two Pairs
Harrison Bayou

Technical Information

Camera Equipment:
-Hasselblad 500C/M with Zeiss lenses: 100mm, 150mm, 250mm
-Linhof Technorama equipped with a 90mm Schneider lens
-Linhof Master Technika 4x5 with Nikon & Schneider lenses:
 90mm, 120mm, 210mm, 360mm & 500mm

Film:
-Kodak T-Max 100 (120 roll film and 4x5 sheet film)

The film is developed in T-Max RS developer diluted 1:9 and processed in a Jobo Autolab ATL-2 Plus

Printing Process:
All prints are made on Kodak Elite Fine Art paper utilizing all grades from grade 1 through grade 4. The paper is developed in Kodak Selectol-soft and Kodak Dektol. Developing times vary depending on contrast control needed to express the initial experience. All of the prints are printed with either a Durst Laborator SM183 or a Beseler 45 MCRX enlarger. Each enlarger is equipped with a cold light head and Nikkor EL lenses. All prints are toned with Selenium and washed to archival standards.

General Notes:
Great care is made to ensure that the initial exposure will be responsive to the printing process. The range of contrasts is controlled by the linkage of the exposure time to the development time and the concentration of the developer. Even though these methods of control are employed at exposure and in the development of the negative it seldom yields a print that will communicate the initial interest.

The printing process remains the most important step in communication. These prints utilize a combination of techniques including the following:

-Variation in the developers and paper grades to control contrast
-Flashing
-Dodging and burning
-Masking with templates
-Bleaching selected areas
-Selected selenium intensification of negatives
-Selenium toning of the final print
-Spotting

Variations in the use and combinations of these techniques are a part of each print. I have found that learning how to print a negative requires a period of contemplation. For me, it is best to spend some time to learn about a negative, then let it rest for a day or two, then with a fresh eye make adjustments. At that point I produce a print that benefits from that pause in the process. A printing session later may yield an enhanced interpretation of the initial experience. A negative cannot be reprinted without bringing to that effort feelings that further develop the initial intent.

The purpose of the printing process is to communicate with the best tools available the expression of that initial experience. The print is the result of the process and should be clear.

LIST OF PLATES